best easy day hikes
Beartooths

Bill Schneider

HELENA, MONTANA

A FALCON GUIDE®

Falcon® Publishing is continually expanding its list of recreational guidebooks. All books include detailed descriptions, accurate maps, and all the information necessary for enjoyable trips. You can order extra copies of this book and get information and prices for other Falcon guidebooks by writing Falcon, P.O. Box 1718, Helena, MT 59624 or calling 1-800-582-2665. Also, please ask for a free copy of our current catalog. Visit our web site at http:\\www.falconguide.com

©1998 by Falcon Publishing Inc., Helena, Montana.

Falcon and FalconGuide are registered trademarks of Falcon Publishing Inc.

All rights reserved, including the right to reproduce this book or parts thereof in any form, except for inclusion of brief quotations in a review.

Printed in Canada.

1 2 3 4 5 6 7 8 9 0 TP 03 02 01 00 99 98

Cover photo by Jon Gnass.

Cataloging-in-Publication Data is on record at the Library of Congress.

CAUTION

Outdoor recreational activities are by their very nature potentially hazardous. All participants in such activities must assume the responsibility for their own actions and safety. The information contained in this guidebook cannot replace sound judgment and good decision-making skills, which helps reduce the risk of exposure, nor does the scope of this book allow for disclosure of all the potential hazards and risks involved in such activities. Learn as much as possible about the outdoor recreational activities in which you participate, prepare for the unexpected, and be cautious. The reward will be a safer and more enjoyable experience.

 Text pages printed on recycled paper.

Contents

Map Legend v
Overview Map vi
Introduction: What is a "best easy" day hike? 1
About the Beartooths 2
Using This Guidebook 3
Ranking the Hikes: Easiest to Hardest 4
Leave No Trace 5

1. Sioux Charley Lake 8
2. Mystic Lake 12
3. Slough Lake 17
4. Elk Lake 19
5. Wild Bill Lake 21
6. Basin Creek Lakes 23
7. Timberline Lake 26
8. West Fork of Rock Creek 28
9. Lake Fork of Rock Creek 30
10. Hellroaring Lakes 33
11. Glacier Lake 37
12. Gardner Lake 41
13. Hauser Lake 43
14. Night Lake 45
15. Beartooth High Lakes 49

16. Beauty Lake 52
17. Claw Lake 55
18. Native Lake 58
19. Crazy Creek Falls 61
20. Kersey Lake 63
21. Lake Vernon 66
22. Rock Island Lake 68
23. Lady of the Lake 70

About the Author 73

Legend

Interstate	🛡00	Picnic Area	⛱
U.S. Highway	00 000	Campground	▲
State or County Road	(00) (000)	Bridge	⋈
Interstate Highway	═══▶	Mine Site	✕
Paved Road	▬▬▶	City Grid	▦
Unpaved Road, Graded	══▶	Cabins/Buildings	■
Unpaved Road, Poor	=====▶	Ranger Station	⛺
Trailhead	○	Elevation	X 9,782 ft.
Main Trail	~~~		
Secondary Trail	- - -	Mountain/Peak	⛰
Trailless Route	······	Falls, Pouroff	─/─
Large River	▬▬▬	Pass/Saddle	)(
River/Creek, Perennial	～	Gate	•—•
Rapids	≈≈	Glacier	≋
Drainage, Intermittent Creek	-·-·-		
Spring	○⁻	Map Orientation	N ↑
Forest/Wilderness/Park Boundary	⌐⌐⌐	Scale	0 — 30 — 60 Miles

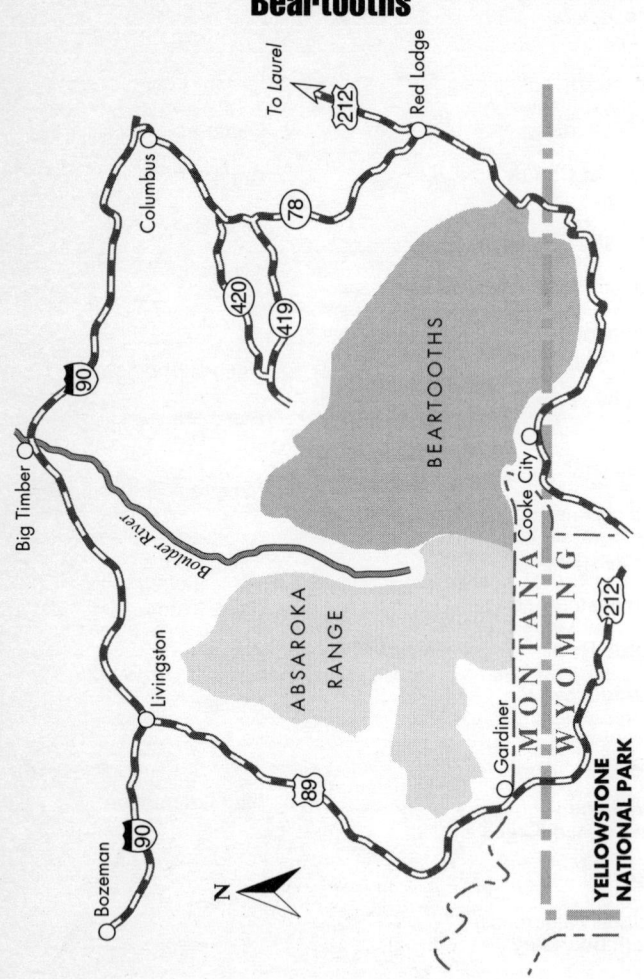

Introduction

What is a "best easy" day hike?

It seems that there are two types of hikers—those who are really serious and those who want an easy day hike. This book is for the second group.

This small book is a much-boiled down version of a larger, more comprehensive book called *Hiking the Beartooths*. This larger book covers every trail in the Beartooths including those that are neither best nor easy. *Best Easy Day Hikes* includes only short, less strenuous hikes that are my recommendations for the nicest day hikes in the Beartooths.

These hikes vary in length, but most are short, although a few are moderate in length. With a few exceptions, none have seriously big hills, and those that do have a serious upgrade are short. In other words, there are no long hikes with big hills. All hikes are on easy-to-follow trails and with one exception (Hellroaring Lakes, Hike 10) there are no off-trail sections.

Some of the hikes in this book might not seem easy to some hikers, but will be easy to others. To help you decide, I've ranked the hikes from easiest to hardest. See page 4. Please keep in mind that short does not always equal easy. Other factors, such as elevation gain and trail conditions, have to be considered.

I hope you thoroughly enjoy your "best easy" hiking in one of America's finest hiking areas.

—*Bill Schneider*

About the Beartooths

A Short Season for Hiking
More than most hiking areas, the Beartooths have only a short hiking season. The high-elevation area usually remains covered with snow into July, and even in July, there is so much water and unmelted snow, hikers can plan on having soaked feet most of the day. The "prime time" to go hiking here is in late July through early September.

Watch the Weather
The Beartooths are widely known for unpredictable weather, and this usually means bad weather. It can snow any day of the year in the Beartooths. Even while on short day hikes, carefully watch the weather, and always be prepared with warm clothing and raingear.

Mosquito Haven
If the conditions are just right (wrong?), the Beartooths can almost disappear under the clouds of mosquitoes, so be prepared with bug dope and mosquito netting. Hiking later in the season (mid-August or later) usually increases your changes of a bug-free trip.

Using this Guidebook

Types of Hikes

Three types of hikes are described in this book:
Loop–Starts and finishes at the same trailhead, with no (or very little) retracing of your steps.
Shuttle–A point-to-point trip that requires two vehicles (one left at the other end of the trail) or a pre-arranged pick up at a designated time and place.
Out-and-back–Traveling to a specific destination, then retracing your steps back to the trailhead.

Type of Maps

Although there are many options for maps, only the following two types are referred to in this book:
USGS–Topographic maps produced by the U.S. Geological Survey.
RMS–Customized topographic maps produced specifically for hikers and anglers by the Rocky Mountain Survey, a private company based in Billings.

Both types of maps are available at local sport stores. RMS maps can be purchased directly from Falcon.

Ranking the Hikes

The following list ranks the hikes in this book from easiest to hardest. No. 1 is the easiest, and No 23 is the hardest.

Easiest
1. Wild Bill Lake
2. Crazy Creek Falls
3. Night Lake
4. Kersey Lake
5. Lake Fork of Rock Creek
6. Hauser Lake
7. Beauty lake
8. Gardner Lake
9. Elk Lake
10. Sioux Charley Lake
11. Rock Island Lake
12. West Fork of Rock Creek
13. Lake Vernon
14. Native Lake
15. Lady of the Lake
16. Basin Creek Lakes
17. Timberline Lake
18. Slough Lake
19. Glacier Lake
20. Mystic Lake
21. Hellroaring Lakes
22. Beartooth High Lakes

Hardest 23. Claw Lake

Leave No Trace

Going into a wilderness area such as the Beartooths is like visiting a famous museum. You obviously do not want to leave your mark on an art treasure in the museum. If everybody going through the museum left one little mark, the piece of art would be quickly destroyed—and of what value is a big building full of trashed art? The same goes for a pristine wilderness such as the Beartooths, which is as magnificent as any masterpiece by any artist. If we all left just one little mark on the landscape, the wilderness would soon be despoiled.

A wilderness can accommodate human use as long as everybody behaves. But a few thoughtless or uninformed visitors can ruin it for everybody who follows. All wilderness users have a responsibility to know and follow the rules of no trace camping. An important source of these guidelines, including the most updated research, can be found in the book *Leave No Trace*. (Ordering information in the back of this book.)

Nowadays most wilderness users want to walk softly, but some aren't aware that they have poor manners. Often their actions are dictated by the outdated habits of a past generation of campers who cut green boughs for evening shelters, built campfires with fire rings, and dug trenches around tents. In the 1950s, these "camping rules" may have been acceptable. But they leave long-lasting scars, and today such behavior is absolutely unacceptable. The wilderness is shrinking, and the number of users is mushrooming. More and more camping areas show unsightly signs of heavy use.

Consequently, a new code of ethics is growing out of the necessity of coping with the unending waves of people who want a perfect wilderness experience. Today, we all must leave no clues that we have gone before. Canoeists can look behind the canoe and see no trace of their passing. Hikers, mountain bikers, and four-wheelers should have the same goal. Enjoy the wildness, but leave no trace of your visit.

Three Falcon Principles of Leave No Trace

- Leave with everything you brought in.
- Leave no sign of your visit.
- Leave the landscape as you found it.

Most of us know better than to litter in or out of the wilderness. Be sure you leave nothing, regardless of how small it is, along the trail or at the campsite. This means you should pack out everything, including orange peels, flip tops, cigarette butts, and gum wrappers. Also, pick up any trash that others leave behind.

Follow the main trail. Avoid cutting switchbacks and walking on vegetation beside the trail.

Don't pick up "souvenirs," such as rocks, antlers, or wildflowers. The next person wants to see them, too, and collecting such souvenirs violates park regulations.

Avoid making loud noises that may disturb others. Remember, sound travels easily to the other side of the lake. Be courteous.

Carry a lightweight trowel to bury human waste 6-8 inches deep and pack out used toilet paper. Keep human waste at least 300 feet from any water source.

Finally, and perhaps most importantly, strictly follow the pack-in/pack-out rule. If you carry something into the backcountry, consume it or carry it out.

Leave no trace—and put your ear to the ground in the wilderness and listen carefully. Thousands of people coming behind you are thanking you for your courtesy and good sense.

1
SIOUX CHARLEY LAKE

Type of hike: Out-and-back.
Total distance: 6 miles.
Maps: USGS, Cathedral Point; RMS, Mount Douglas-Mount Wood.
Finding the trailhead: From Interstate 90 at Columbus, drive 15 miles south on Montana Highway 78 to Absarokee. Continue south 2 miles and turn west on the paved Nye Road (County Road 419), and go through Fishtail and Nye. Stay on this road, which eventually ends at the trailhead, about 2 miles past the Stillwater Mine. It's about 42 miles southwest of Columbus.

Overview: The Stillwater River Trailhead is one of the most accessible and heavily used access points to the Beartooths. It's also a large trailhead with toilet facilities and plenty of parking and a large Forest Service campground.

Getting there is a treat. The drive up the Stillwater River is one of the most scenic in Montana. The Stillwater River flows majestically through a landscape dominated by large ranches interspersed with small ranching communities like Fishtail, Nye, Beehive, Dean, and Moraine.

The Stillwater River carries more water out of the Beartooths than any other stream, and it's certainly one of the most beautiful drainages. Nowadays, however, it is a little less wild than in the recent past. The north rim of the Beartooths, and especially the Stillwater River area, is highly mineralized. In recent years, several large mining developments have sprung up in this area. The rapid growth of mines

Sioux Charley Lake

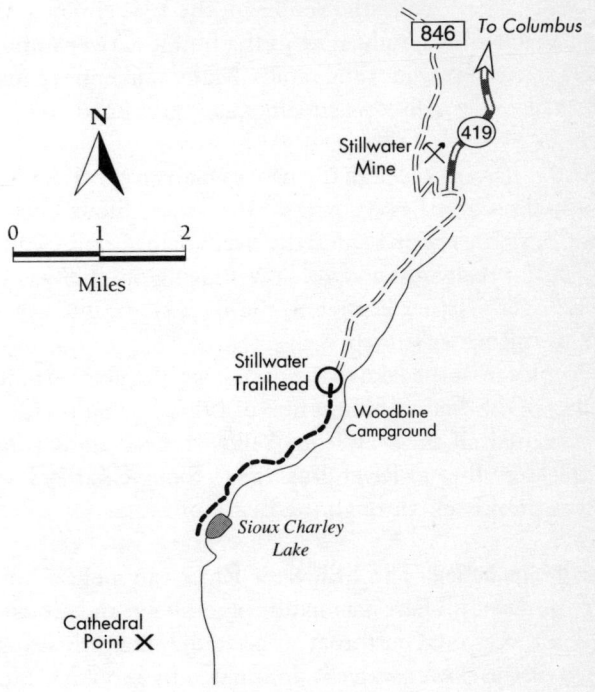

and the associated residential development has brought many more people into this remote part of Montana.

The hike: The trip into Sioux Charley Lake is one of the most popular day hikes in the Beartooths, so don't be surprised to see lots of people on the trail. From the trailhead, it's 3 miles to the lake, all on an easy, slightly uphill grade.

Soon after leaving the trailhead, the trail enters a narrow canyon where, right next to the trail, the river tumbles over a series of cascades and rapids. Many a hiker has paused here to wonder why this stream was ever named the "still water."

After passing through the narrow canyon the trail winds its way through a heavy forest all the way to Sioux Charley Lake. Now the reason behind the river's name becomes clear. The lake is really just a large, slow-moving or "still" section of the river. Farther upstream, the river slows into several similar still-water stretches.

Look across the lake to the east to see the northernmost reaches of the dramatic forest fires of 1988. The Storm Creek Fire burned all the way from Yellowstone National Park down the Stillwater River drainage to Sioux Charley Lake, almost completely through the Beartooths.

Fishing information: The Stillwater River can yield a lot of pan-sized trout. There is a mixture of rainbows and brookies, with an occasional cutthroat to be found along this route. Much of the slower water is dominated by brookies. Since brook trout tend to overpopulate (to the detriment of other species), please eat them and help out the cutts and rainbows. Catch and release doesn't improve the brookies' size—it only limits the amount of food per fish. Besides, they taste great! Sioux Charley Lake is one of the best places to catch these tasty morsels, and the omnipresent brookies can provide dinner for many large parties.

2
MYSTIC LAKE

Type of hike: Out-and-back.
Total distance: 7 miles.
Maps: USGS, Granite Peak and Alpine; RMS, Cooke City–Cutoff Mountain.
Finding the trailhead: To find the West Rosebud Trailhead, drive 15 miles south from Columbus on Montana Highway 78 to Absarokee. Continue through Absarokee about 2 miles and turn right (west) to Fishtail. Drive through Fishtail and go west and south about 1 mile. Turn left (south) along the West Rosebud Road. About 6 miles later, take another left (southeast) at the sign for West Rosebud Lake. It's another 14 miles of bumpy gravel road from this point to the trailhead. In total, it's 27 miles from Absarokee and 42 miles from Columbus. The road ends and the trail begins right at the Mystic Dam Power Station.

There is a spacious parking lot and toilet facilities at the trailhead. But it might not seem clear exactly where the trail begins. After parking your vehicle, walk up the road about 200 yards through the Montana Power Company compound to the actual trailhead.

Overview: The West Rosebud Trailhead is one of the most unusual in the Beartooths. The trail starts in a Montana Power Company work area, and for the first 2 miles or so it climbs to a manmade dam on Mystic Lake. The dam raised the water level of the natural lake, making Mystic the deepest lake in the Beartooths (more than 200 feet). Plus, two delightful lakes—Emerald and West Rosebud—lie right at the trailhead.

Located about 80 miles southwest of Billings, the West Rosebud is similar to the East Rosebud and other trailheads on the northern face of the Beartooths. The gravel access road follows a beautiful stream (West Rosebud Creek) through traditional Montana ranching country, mostly undeveloped. The road may be rough in sections, but it can be negotiated easily by any two-wheel-drive vehicle. Besides, the scenery is well worth the bumps. Travelers can see the narrow valley opening up in the mountains long before they arrive.

This area also resembles East Rosebud because of the little community at the trailhead. Instead of summer cabins, however, the structures at this trailhead house workers employed by the owner of Mystic Dam Power Station, the Montana Power Company.

The West Rosebud is the only major drainage in the Beartooths that's closed to horse traffic during the summer. This is due to hazardous rock fields and snowdrifts common on a section of trail just before Mystic Lake early in the season. Horses are allowed into the area, however, during the fall big-game hunting seasons, usually starting in mid-September.

A short way up the trail, look for a plaque placed in a stone in memory of Mark E. Von Seggern, a Boy Scout

Mystic Lake, Slough Lake, Elk Lake

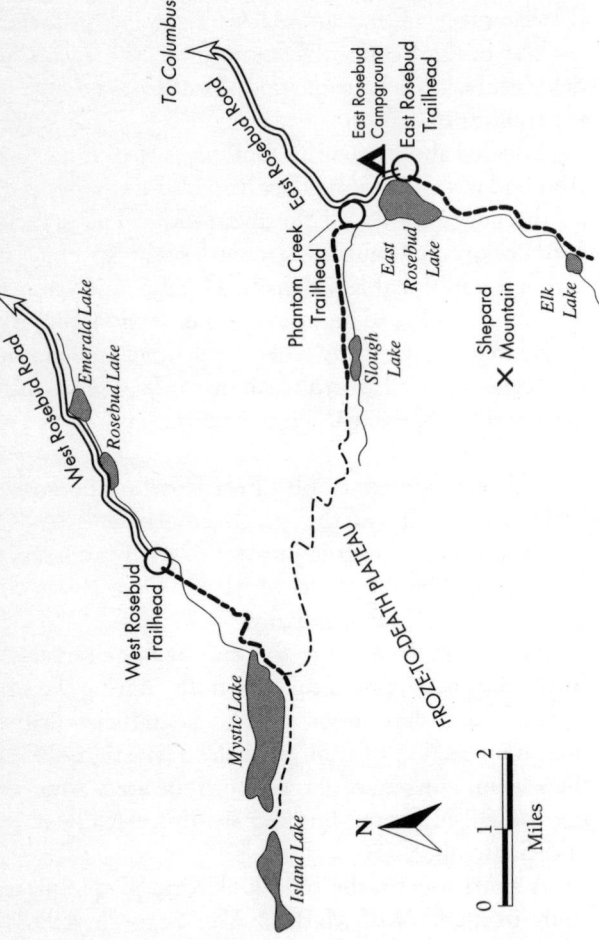

from Columbus who died in 1979 after a tragic slide down a snowbank near Mystic Lake.

The plaque also offers that age-old (but never out-of-date) advice: "Be Prepared." This is especially true for weekend adventurers heading up to Froze-to-Death Plateau to climb Montana's highest mountain, Granite Peak. Actually, Granite isn't a difficult climb for experienced climbers, but many people going up the mountain aren't that experienced. Perhaps the plaque will remind them that at least they should be prepared.

The hike: For those who aren't interested in strenuous mountain climbing or long arduous trips, the Mystic Lake Trail offers an excellent choice for an unhurried day in the wilderness. It also offers some spectacular scenery with the unusual twist of being able to observe how the Mystic Lake Power Station was built.

Besides being a popular day trip, this is also the major launching point for the legions that attempt to climb Granite Peak each year. Don't expect to have the trail to yourself.

After crossing an overpass and a bridge over West Rosebud Creek, the trail follows a power line for a short way. After leaving this "sign of civilization" behind, the trail switchbacks through open rock fields, offering a great view of the West Rosebud valley, including West Rosebud and Emerald lakes below.

The climb doesn't seem that steep, but by the time the trail reaches the dam, it has ascended 1,200 feet in 3 miles. Normally, that would be considered a big climb, but for hikers who aren't in a hurry, it really doesn't seem like it.

When the trail finally breaks out over the ridge, it affords a great view of Mystic Dam. Mystic Lake is a natural lake, but the dam increased its size and depth. The sandy beach along the east shore of the lake below is perhaps the largest in the Beartooths.

This makes a good lunch spot for those who plan to turn back for the trailhead. But it's far better to set aside enough time to walk along the lake for a while. The trail is very scenic, flat, and well maintained. It's difficult to realize the full scope of Mystic Lake from the first overlook. This is a huge lake, and a walk along its shore is the best way to appreciate this fact.

Some people might think that the presence of the dam detracts from the wildness of the place. But Montana Power Company has done as much as possible to keep the intrusion to a minimum, and after all, the dam was here long before the Absaroka-Beartooths was designated as wilderness. At any rate, most visitors have little difficulty enjoying the scenery and fresh air.

Fishing information: There are a lot of fish willing to be caught near the trailhead at Emerald and West Rosebud lakes. Both lakes support hefty fish with brown trout, cutthroat trout, and whitefish all common. Rainbows are stocked in both lakes, to provide some additional excitement.

Mystic Lake supports a rainbow trout fishery that is great when the fish are feeding and frustrating when they are not, although the fickle rainbows found there can usually be coaxed. The rainbows can be counted on for a good workout. The stream up to Mystic is very steep and doesn't provide great habitat for fish, so save your effort for the lake.

3
SLOUGH LAKE

> see map on page 14

Type of hike: Out-and-back.
Total distance: 4 miles.
Maps: USGS, Alpine; RMS, Alpine–Mount Maurice.
Finding the trailhead: From Interstate 90 at Columbus, drive south 29 miles on Montana Highway 78 to Roscoe. Drive into this small ranching community, being careful not to stop at the Grizzly Bar—until the return trip of course, when you'll be really ready for the famous "Grizzly Burger." At the north end of Roscoe the road turns to gravel and goes about 14.5 miles to the East Rosebud Trailhead. About 7 miles from Roscoe the road crosses East Rosebud Creek and forks. Take a sharp right and continue south along the creek. The road is mostly gravel except a 4-mile paved section near the end. There are three trailheads at East Rosebud Lake. Phantom Creek Trail 17 begins on the right (west) side of the road about 0.3 mile before the lake. This is a popular route to Froze-to-Death Plateau and Granite Peak.

Overview: Many people who know the Beartooths say the East Rosebud is the most scenic valley of all. It's filled with lakes and waterfalls that would be major tourism attractions anywhere else. Here, there are so many, most don't even have names. The cutthroat-filled lakes bring a smile to any angler's face, and climbers love the place because of the endless array of rock faces. Consequently, the East Rosebud

Trailhead is probably the largest and most heavily used in the Beartooths.

Adding even more use to the area is the small community of summer homes called Alpine right at the trailhead. The summer homes extend up both sides of the lower sections of East Rosebud Lake, closing off much of the lake to public use.

The hike: This trail is perfectly suited for a leisurely, quiet day in the wilderness amid some great scenery.

Trail 17 climbs, with gradual switchbacks, along Armstrong Creek for about 2 miles to Slough Lake. This is a gorgeous, glacier-carved cirque, and Slough Lake sits in the midst of it like a little pearl. Actually, there are two small lakes.

Even though this trail receives heavy use, few people take their time along here or even stop at Slough Lake. Most are rushing to the top of Froze-to-Death Plateau to climb Granite Peak. Lucky for the rest of us that they hurry right by this pastoral pond, a perfect spot to sit on a sunny day savoring the spirit of the wilderness.

If you want a little more exercise, hike about another 0.5 mile until the trail breaks out of the forest. This gives you a truly spectacular vista highlighted by Hole-in-the-Wall Mountain to the left (south) and Froze-to-Death Plateau to the west.

Fishing information: Slough Lake provides a good source of willing brookies for dinner.

4
ELK LAKE

see map on page 14

Type of hike: Out-and-back.
Total distance: 6 miles.
Maps: USGS, Alpine; RMS, Alpine–Mount Maurice.
Finding the trailhead: Same general directions as detailed under the Slough Lake hike. However, instead of stopping at the Phantom Creek Trailhead, continue on around the east side of East Rosebud Lake and the community of Alpine past the campground to the end of the road which is also the trailhead for Trail 15 heading up the East Rosebud.

Overview: Refer to Slough Lake, Hike 3.

The hike: This trail covers the first 3 miles of the popular trans-Beartooth trail from East Rosebud to Cooke City, sometimes referred to as "The Beaten Path." The trail is well-maintained and well-traveled. Expect to see lots of people.

The trail starts at the huge East Rosebud Trailhead and goes through a forested valley all the way to Elk Lake. In 1996, a forest fire burned through here, so expect to see the aftermath of the fire.

Along the trail you can also get several great views of 10,979-foot Shepard Mountain to the west and East Rosebud Creek as it tumbles down from the Beartooth Plateau.

Elk Lake is nestled in a forested pocket just below the point where the trail starts to traverse more rocky, open terrain. The upper end of the lake has a pleasant spot for lunch.

Fishing information: Elk Lake offers both cutthroat and brook trout fishing with the brook trout providing the largest portion of a possible dinner. Anglers day hiking to Elk Lake should plan a couple of stops to fish in the creek. East Rosebud Lake holds some large brown trout, along with a mixed bag of brookies, rainbows, and cutthroats.

5
WILD BILL LAKE

Type of hike: Loop.
Total distance: 1 mile.
Maps: No maps needed.
Finding the trailhead: Turn west on the West Fork of Rock Creek Road (Forest Road 71), which leaves U.S. Highway 212 on the south end of Red Lodge. After 2.7 miles, the road bends left and heads up the West Fork. After driving another 3.3 miles on the paved road, turn right (north) into the well-signed parking lot for Wild Bill Lake.

Overview: Refer to Basin Creek Lakes, Hike 6.

The hike: Wild Bill Lake was built by "Wild Bill" Kurtzer with a hand-built dam. He stocked fish in the small lake and rented fishing boats to tourists. He built quite a commercial venture and even had a heated swimming hole.

A delightful short trail follows the shoreline all around Wild Bill Lake. Part of the trail is accessible to wheelchairs. The lake is still stocked with trout. This is a great short hike for people with small children.

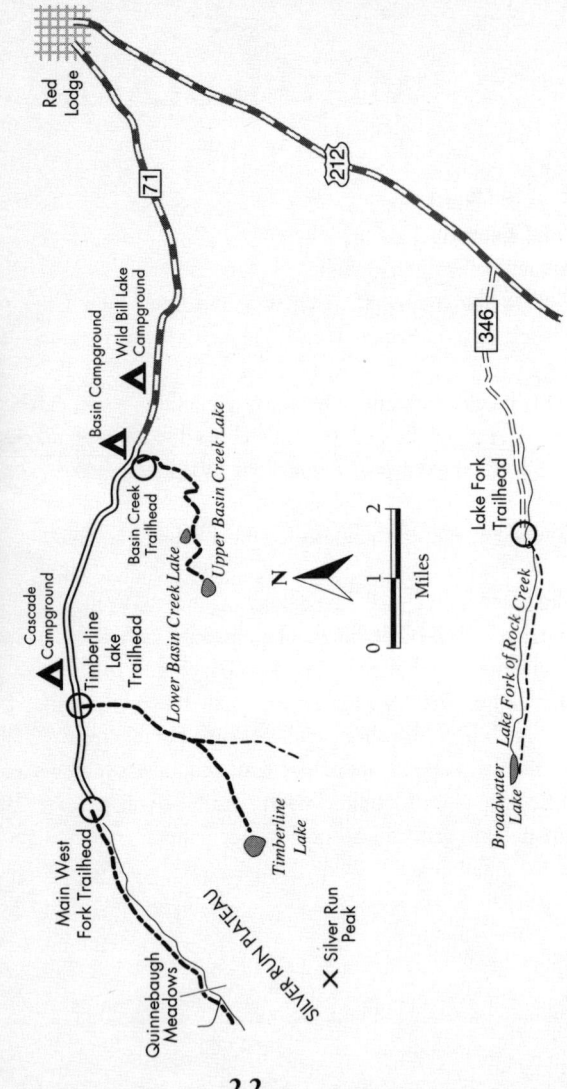

6
BASIN CREEK LAKES

see map on page 22

Type of hike: Out and back.
Total distance: 5 miles to lower lake, 8 miles to upper lake.
Maps: USGS—Bare Mountain; RMS—Alpine-Mount Maurice.
Finding the trailhead: Turn west on the West Fork of Rock Creek Road (Forest Road 71), which leaves U.S. Highway 212 on the south end of Red Lodge. After 2.7 miles, the road bends left and heads up the West Fork. The first of four trailheads is Basin Creek, 7 miles from Red Lodge.

Key points:
0.5 Basin Creek Falls.
2.5 Lower Basin Creek Lake.
4.0 Upper Basin Creek Lake.

Overview: The West Fork of Rock Creek Road (FR 71) actually boasts four separate trailheads, all in close proximity. Three vehicle campgrounds are also found in this area, and the lower valley has several residential developments. Since the road starts right in Red Lodge, the lower valley is almost like part of the town's backyard wilderness.

The West Fork road is paved for the first 7 miles up to Basin Campground. This is a heavily used area, both for day trips and extended backcountry excursions. Fortunately, the area offers a wide range of trail choices and visitors tend to disperse. Trails rarely feel crowded.

The hike: The Forest Service has designated Basin Creek as a National Recreational Trail, so not surprisingly, it's a popular hike. It's so popular, in fact, that this is one of the few trails in the Beartooths restricted to hiking only—no horses are allowed until mid-September when the big game hunting seasons get underway.

Technically, Trail 61 to Basin Creek Lakes does not lie within the Absaroka-Beartooth Wilderness, but it's a wilderness trip by all other definitions. The trail is well maintained, easy to follow and ideal for family day trips for those who can handle the gradual, but steady uphill gradient. The route crosses Basin Creek twice, but bridges keep your feet dry.

About 0.5 mile up the trail, listen for Basin Creek Falls tumbling down from above. Where the trail takes a sharp right, hikers can scramble up a short, undeveloped spur trail to get a closer look at the falls, which is well worth the short detour. The rest of the trail is hazard-free, but this short climb up to see the falls might be too hazardous for small children.

The trail passes through thick forest all the way. With so much of the Beartooths burned by the 1988 fires, this peaceful walk in the woods can be a real treat. The remains of past logging activity from the early 1900s are still visible along the way—but it's also apparent that nature is finally reclaiming the disturbed landscape.

Lower Basin Lake is one of those forest-lined mountain ponds with darkish, warm water that tends to be half-covered by lily pads. Upper Basin Lake is larger, deeper, and nestled in a picturesque mountain cirque.

Fishing information: While both of these lakes once supported brook trout populations, the lower lake suffered a freeze-out a few years back and currently has no fish. Since the brook trout in the stream and lake above will eventually work their way back down to Lower Basin, there is no immediate need to restock. Fishing in Upper Basin Lake is excellent for brook trout, and there has been some talk of introducing grayling.

7
TIMBERLINE LAKE

see map on page 22

Type of hike: Out-and-back
Total distance: 9 miles.
Maps: USGS, Sylvan Peak and Bare Mountain; RMS, Alpine–Mount Maurice.
Finding the trailhead: Turn west on the West Fork of Rock Creek Road (FR 71), which leaves U.S. Highway 212 on the south end of Red Lodge. After 2.7 miles, the road bends left and heads up the West Fork. The first of four trailheads is Basin Creek, 7 miles from Red Lodge, followed by Timberline Lakes at 10.7 miles.

Key points:
3.0 Junction with Beartrack Trail 8.
4.0 Lake Gertrude.
4.5 Timberline Lake.

Overview: Refer to Basin Creek Lakes, Hike 6.

The hike: Similar to the nearby trail up Basin Creek, the trail to Timberline Lake passes through a forested environment. Here, however, the forest is more open and mature than along Basin Creek. As with almost all trails in the Custer National Forest section of the Absaroka-Beartooth Wilderness, this one is well maintained and marked.

get FALCON GUIDED

FALCONGUIDES are the ultimate in recreational guidebooks. Each guide provides comprehensive information on trails, trips, and the best places to go in each state. Detailed descriptions are accompanied by maps, access information, photos, and safety tips. Regularly updated and revised, FALCONGUIDES provide the most current, accurate information possible. Whatever you do outside, use a FALCONGUIDE to plan your next trip into the great outdoors.

FALCONGUIDES are available for:
Hiking, Rock Climbing, Rockhounding, Mountain Biking, Scenic Driving, Watching Wildlife, Fishing and more.

MORE THAN 4 MILLION COPIES SOLD!

To locate your nearest retailer call
1-800-582-2665.
Also use this number for
a complete list of Falcon titles including
books on nature and the West.
**For a FREE catalog, return this card with
the following information.**

Name _____
Address _____
City _____
State _____ Zip _____

☐ **YES!** I'd like to send a catalog to a friend.

Name _____
Address _____
City _____
State _____ Zip _____

FALCON

BUSINESS REPLY MAIL
FIRST-CLASS MAIL PERMIT NO. 80 HELENA MT

POSTAGE WILL BE PAID BY THE ADDRESSEE

FALCON PUBLISHING CO INC
PO BOX 1718
HELENA MT 59624-9917

**NO POSTAGE
NECESSARY
IF MAILED
IN THE
UNITED STATES**

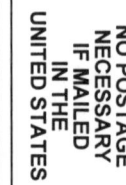

The corridor to Timberline Lake was excluded from the Absaroka-Beartooth Wilderness. However, Lake Gertrude and Timberline Lake lie within the wilderness boundary, and current wilderness bills call for adding the corridor to the wilderness.

It's a short 3 miles to the junction with Beartrack Trail 8, which veers off to the left and heads up to Silver Run Plateau. Turn right and continue along Timberline Creek. If you cross the stream here, you took a wrong turn.

After another mile or so, look for Lake Gertrude nestled in a forested pocket off to the right. This is a good spot to pause for a rest while enjoying Lake Gertrude, which also marks the boundary of the Absaroka-Beartooth Wilderness. Don't burn too much daylight here, however—Timberline Lake is only 0.5 mile farther and the basin is definitely worth exploring.

The view from Timberline Lake is fantastic, especially to the south toward Timberline Glacier and 12,500-foot Silver Run Peak. Adventuresome hikers might want to try a side trip up to the glacier.

Fishing information: Both lakes along this trail have healthy populations of brook trout. The fish aren't large, but can probably be counted on to provide dinner.

8
WEST FORK OF ROCK CREEK

see map on page 22

Type of hike: Out-and-back.
Total distance: Up to 10 miles.
Maps: USGS, Sylvan Peak and Bare Mountain; RMS, Alpine–Mount Maurice.
Finding the trailhead: Turn west on the West Fork of Rock Creek Road (Forest Road 71), which leaves U.S. Highway 212 on the south end of Red Lodge. After 2.7 miles, the road bends left and heads up the West Fork. The trailhead for this hike is at the end of the road, 14 miles from Red Lodge.

Key points:
1.3 Calamity Falls.
1.1 Sentinel Falls.
5.0 Quinnebaugh Meadows and junction with Lake Mary Trail.

Overview: Refer to Basin Creek Lakes, Hike 6.

The hike: The trail, like others in this region, is well maintained and marked. It closely follows the West Fork, not climbing any more than the stream drops in elevation as it powers its way out of the Beartooths. Most of the trail passes through a rich forest that gradually thins out as you progress up the drainage. In a few places, the forest opens up into small meadows with rewarding vistas of Elk Mountain and Bowback Mountain on the southern horizon near the terminus of the West Fork valley.

The trail passes close by Calamity Falls and Sentinel Falls. These cascades are reminders that the West Fork is not only a peaceful stream meandering out of the wilderness, but it can be a powerful force. Short spur trails lead to both falls for better views.

The West Fork broadens out and slows down just as the trail nears Quinnebaugh Meadows. Look for the sign for Lake Mary just after breaking out into the enormous mountain meadow. This is a popular place, so expect company.

Fishing information: Although the West Fork of Rock Creek is not highly productive, anglers can find a few trout in many stretches of this stream. The stream near Quinnebaugh Meadows is no exception. The best fishing, however, is found in various basin lakes 1,000 feet higher in elevation.

9
LAKE FORK OF ROCK CREEK

Type of hike: Out-and-back.
Total distance: Up to 7 miles (round-trip distance to Broadwater Lake).
Maps: USGS, Black Pyramid Mountain; RMS, Alpine-Mount Maurice.
Finding the trailhead: From Red Lodge drive southwest for about 10 miles on U.S. Highway 212. Turn west at the well-marked road up the Lake Fork of Rock Creek. A short, paved road leads to a turnaround and the trailhead.

Overview: The Lake Fork of Rock Creek area is similar to the West Fork, just to the north. Both areas are easily accessible from Red Lodge and receive lots of use. This high level of use in the Lake Fork may be even more obvious because everybody uses the same trail. In the West Fork, multiple trails tend to disperse the use.

The hike: This well-maintained and heavily used trail is not only one of the most scenic in the Beartooths, but it's only a short drive from the Billings area. This trail offers absolutely spectacular scenery.

From the trailhead, immediately cross a bridge over the Lake Fork of Rock Creek, turn right (west), and head upstream along the Lake Fork. The trail stays close to the stream all the way. You can go all the way to Broadwater Lake or turn back whenever you've had all the awesome scenery you can take for one day.

The trail is easy to follow, well maintained, hazard-free, and usually dry. Plus, there are no steep hills to climb. The trail stays on the south side of the stream the entire way to Broadwater Lake.

All of these advantages make this trip near-perfect for an easy day hike with children. Perhaps the best part of the trip into Broadwater Lake is constantly being near a clean, natural mountain stream. Hikers can stop dozens of places and just sit back against a tree, relax, and soak in the sound of the rushing water.

Along the way, watch for water ouzels playing in the blue green waters of the Lake Fork. Also, expect to see lots of wildflowers along the stream.

Lake Fork of Rock Creek

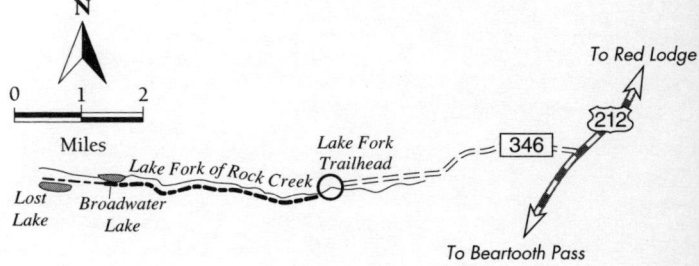

Broadwater Lake is beautiful, but not well-named. It's not really a lake at all, but a long "glide" where the stream widens and slows for a few moments before hurrying out of the mountains.

Fishing information: Like the West Fork, the Lake Fork of Rock Creek is exceptionally photogenic, but it supports fewer fish than might be expected. The cold water, restricted sunlight, and fast current don't make life easy for fish. The Lake Fork supports both cutthroat and brook trout, but with some exceptions the numbers are not high. Fish concentrate in the slower sections of the stream, and Broadwater Lake is one of these.

10
HELLROARING LAKES

Type of hike: Out-and-back or small loop.
Total distance: 4 to 8 miles, depending on how much exploring you do.
Maps: USGS, Black Pyramid Mountain; RMS, Alpine–Mount Maurice.
Finding the trailhead: Drive south from Red Lodge on U.S. Highway 212 for about 12 miles. Watch for a well-marked turnoff on the right (west) at Hellroaring Creek to three Forest Service campgrounds. This road enters the campground maze, but everything is well signed. The roads to the two trailheads start immediately after a bridge across from the entrance to Limberpine Campground. After driving over the bridge across from the entrance to Limberpine Campground take a short jog to the right on a well-signed road and start switchbacking up the ridge. The rocky road to the Hellroaring Trailhead climbs up a steep slope for about 6 miles. A high-clearance vehicle is needed to get over the sharp rocks and around the tight switchbacks. The last 0.25 mile to the trailhead gets very rough. The road ends on the edge of Hellroaring Plateau.

Overview: The Rock Creek area is the last stop before driving up the world-famous switchbacks to the top of Beartooth Pass and into Wyoming. Actually, there are two trailheads

(Glacier Lake and Hellroaring) in the area, both accessed from the Forest Service campgrounds at the base of Beartooth Pass. Day hikers can camp at one of the three vehicle campgrounds and go to Hellroaring Lakes and Glacier Lake on extended one-day outings.

A high-clearance vehicle is needed to get to the trailheads. Snow usually blocks these gravel roads until July.

The hike: The trails in this area are great for learning to explore the high country with a topo map and compass, and they are especially well suited for hikers who aren't in animal-like physical condition. Many lakes and other scenic areas can be reached within a few miles of the trailhead. The climbs can be steep, but not extended.

From the trailhead, follow an old, closed-off jeep road about 1 mile along the Hellroaring Plateau. Lower Hellroaring Lakes are soon visible in the valley off to the right (north). You are better off continuing on along the plateau instead of going down to the lakes from this point. If you drop off too early, the terrain gets very steep and it's a fight through a maze of alpine willows and small streams.

Instead, continue along the plateau for another 0.5 mile or so. The scenery is worth it. Wander over to the south edge of the plateau on the left to see the main fork of Rock Creek.

At about the 1.5-mile mark and just before a huge snowbank on the right (northwest), head down to the lakes. Take a close look at the topo map before dropping off the plateau and keep the map handy until you climb back out of the basin.

Hellroaring Lakes, Glacier Lake

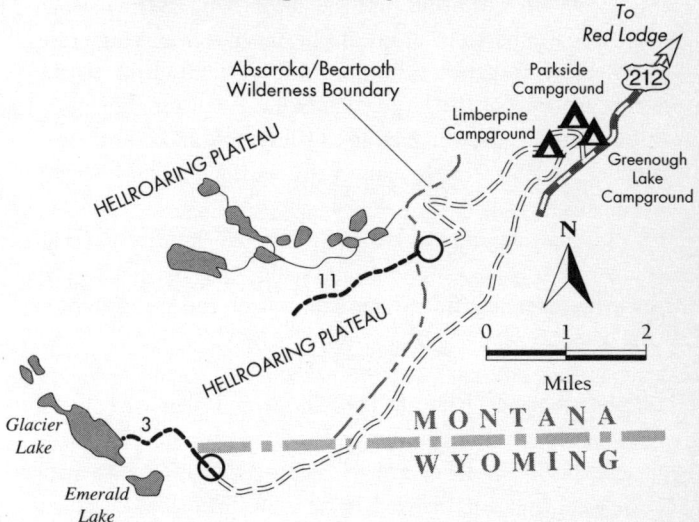

The climb down to the lakes is more gradual from this point. Watch for game trails on the way down, but be prepared for essentially off-trail hiking. Once at the lakes, the hiking is much easier. There are fairly well-defined angler's trails between the lakes.

This is a heavenly basin filled with lakes, mostly above 10,000 feet. Hairpin Lake, for example, is definitely worth seeing. It has a series of beautiful bays, and a waterfall plunges into the lake from the northwest. There's plenty of grand places to explore and all within a short distance.

After a few hours exploring the basin, climb back up to the plateau and back to your vehicle. To make a short loop out of the trip, hike down to the lower lakes and then up to the plateau. Bear in mind that the climb back to the plateau from the lower basin is tough. It's better to retrace your steps up the valley and then take the more gradual climb to the plateau just east of the large snowbank. Another short loop can be made by heading west to Sliderock Lake and then climbing back to the plateau on the west side of the snowbank.

While exploring the basin, watch the weather. It's all too easy—and dangerous—to get caught on the plateau by one of the severe thunderstorms that often roll through here in the afternoon.

Fishing information: Three of the Hellroaring Lakes are fishless, and please leave them that way. If you're prepared for mosquitoes, the lower lakes are the perfect place to take your son or daughter for his or her first mountain lake fishing trip. Each small lake has its own personality, and most support brook trout and cutthroat trout. The trees here provide cover from the wind and a visual break from the rocky terrain above.

When you're tired of catching the numerous smaller trout in the lower lakes, head up the drainage. Hairpin Lake has nice cutts, some of which could break a line. On the way back out, make the side trip to Sliderock Lake for some of the healthiest brook trout anywhere in the Beartooths.

11
GLACIER LAKE

> see map on page 35

Type of hike: Out-and-back.
Total distance: 4 miles, plus side trips.
Maps: USGS, Beartooth Butte and Silver Run Peak; RMS, Alpine–Mount Maurice and Wyoming Beartooths.
Finding the trailhead: Drive south from Red Lodge on U.S. Highway 212 for about 12 miles. Watch for a well-marked turnoff on the right (west) at Hellroaring Creek to three Forest Service campgrounds. This road enters the campground maze, but everything is well signed. The roads to the two trailheads start immediately after a bridge across from the entrance to Limberpine Campground. To get to the Glacier Lake Trailhead, turn left (southwest) on the clearly signed gravel road just after crossing the bridge by the entrance to Limberpine Campground. Once on the correct road, there's no chance of getting off it because there are no other forks or spur roads. It's a long, slow 8 miles to the trailhead. Most of the road can be traversed by a passenger car, but a high-clearance vehicle is essential for the last 0.5 mile or so.

Overview: Refer to Hellroaring Lakes, Hike 10.

The hike: The Glacier Lake area seems nicely suited to a long day of exploring, fishing, photographing, and simply enjoying high-elevation majestic vistas. It's easily accessible by a 2-mile trail. The Forest Service has restricted stock use on this trail due to hazardous conditions for horses.

The trail to Glacier Lake is short but very steep. The trailhead is at 8,680 feet and the lake is at 9,702 feet, but the route actually climbs more than the difference (1,022 feet) in the 2 miles to Glacier Lake. That's because there's a ridge in the middle that's about 800 feet higher than the lake.

After climbing for about 0.5 mile, the trail crosses Moon Creek on a bridge. After Moon Creek, the trail gets even steeper—and the higher it goes, the better the scenery gets.

Shortly after Moon Creek, a faint, unofficial trail veers off to the north to Moon Lake and Shelf Lake. Turn left (west) and stay on what is obviously the main trail. For most of the way, the trail is rough and rock-studded, but it remains easy to follow and without hazards.

Once atop the ridge, you cross some rock shelves on your way down to massive Glacier Lake. Even though the lake sits at 9,702 feet (above timberline), some large trees stand along the shoreline.

The trail reaches the lake at a small dam built long ago to increase the depth of Glacier Lake. A faint trail heads off to the right and goes about halfway around the lake. After a large point jutting out into the lake, the trail degenerates into a series of boulder fields and talus slopes. Watch for the amazing numbers of pikas that inhabit the area.

Bearing right along the north shore of the lake affords views of Triangle Lake and access to Mountain Sheep Lake and Mountain Goat Lake at the head of the basin.

Bearing left and across the dam around the south shore of the lake leads directly to Little Glacier Lake, a small jewel just barely separated from Glacier Lake. Continuing south on this trail over a small ridge treats wanderers to the sight of lovely Emerald Lake. Early in the season, you might have to get your feet wet wading the outlet stream of Glacier Lake to get to Emerald Lake.

Because of topography, Glacier Lake tends to become remarkably windy during mid-day, so try to arrive early to catch the scenery before the winds start ripping through this valley. Emerald Lake is not quite as windy.

Fishing information: Anglers must be sure to keep track of which state you're in, and make sure you have the right license. The state line goes right through Glacier Lake. Little Glacier and Emerald lakes are in Wyoming.

The ice-cold water, high-canyon walls, and swift-running water make Rock Creek extremely attractive to look at, but these conditions also make life hard for fish. Rock Creek is home to small populations of cutthroat and brook trout. Fish concentrate in the slower water, so look for good holding places out of the current. The main fork of Rock Creek winds in and out of Wyoming and Montana, so anglers need to know which state they're in and have the appropriate license.

Glacier Lake supports cutthroat and brook trout, both of which grow to above-average size. The fish tend to school, with cutthroats working rocky shorelines, so anglers should work the shoreline as well. When water levels are high, water flows between Glacier and Little Glacier lakes, so the fishery is the same in both. But the fish are easier to find in Little Glacier. Emerald Lake supports both cutts and brookies as well, though they are slightly smaller than those in Glacier.

Cutts are stocked in Mountain Goat Lake and work their way down to Mountain Sheep Lake. Count on more fish in the upper lake and larger ones in the lower.

12
GARDNER LAKE

Type of hike: Out-and-back.
Total distance: 1.5 miles.
Maps: USGS, Deep Lake; RMS, Wyoming Beartooths.
Finding the trailhead: The trailhead is a large pull out on the south side of the Beartooth Highway about 35 miles east of Cooke City and 28 miles west of Red Lodge.

Overview: The undesignated wilderness south of the Beartooth Highway is often ignored as hikers flock to the more well-known trails north of the road. Yet, the area south of the highway is equally wild and scenic and, of course, less crowded.

Gardner Lake

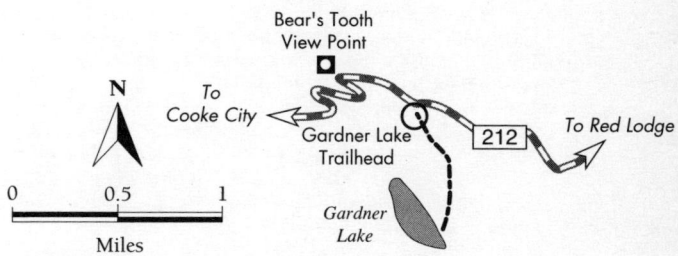

The hike: The trail to Gardner Lake is the beginning of the Beartooth Loop National Recreation Trail, a long backpacking route.

Gardner Lake is the fairly large lake you can see from the trailhead. You can also see that even though it's only 0.75 mile to the lake, it's all downhill to get there and all uphill to get back to your vehicle.

This is high country. The trail starts at 10,936 feet and drops to 9,950 feet at the lake. This elevation prevents tree growth, so the entire hike goes through open alpine terrain. Along the trail you can note many species of delicate alpine wildflowers.

After relaxing at the lake for awhile, take a deep breath before slowly heading back up the 600-foot climb to the trailhead.

13
HAUSER LAKE

Type of hike: Out-and-back.
Total distance: 1.5 miles.
Maps: USGS, Deep Lake; RMS, Wyoming Beartooths.
Finding the trailhead: The trailhead is a small pull out on the north side of the Beartooth Highway along Long Lake about 29 miles east of Cooke City and 37 miles southwest of Red Lodge.

Overview: Refer to Gardner Lake, Hike 12.

The hike: This is similar to the Gardner Lake hike without the big hill.

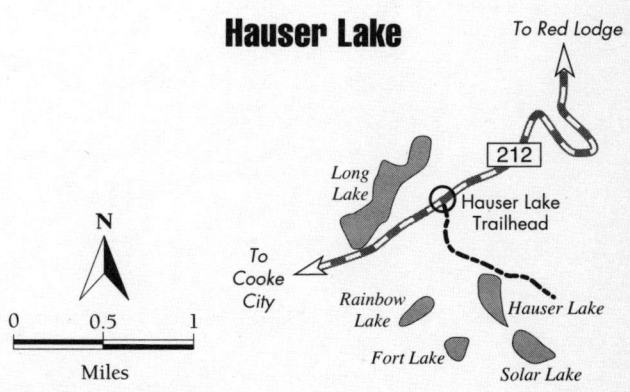

The trail is not well defined in the meadow along the road, so keep your eyes peeled for a few big cairns that mark the presence of the trail. Once you get near the trees, the trail becomes easy to follow and stays that way all the way to Hauser Lake. The elevation on this hike is much lower in elevation than the trail to Gardner Lake—starting at 9,841 feet and going to the lake at 9,650 feet. The area is mostly open—and very scenic.

If you have some extra time and energy (and don't mind off-trail hiking), you can visit three more lakes with very short walks from Hauser Lake: Solar, Fort, and Rainbow lakes.

Fishing information: All four lakes have fair fishing, but make sure you have a Wyoming fishing license.

14
NIGHT LAKE

Type of hike: Out-and-back.
Total distance: 2 miles.
Maps: USGS, Beartooth Butte; RMS, Wyoming Beartooths.
Finding the trailhead: The trailhead is easy to find. It's well marked and located at the end of the access road to Island Lake Campground on the west side of Beartooth Pass. From Cooke City, drive about 25 miles east on U.S. Highway 212 and watch for the turn off on the right. From Red Lodge, it's about a 38-mile drive.

Overview: This trailhead is officially named "Island Lake Trailhead," but perhaps a more appropriate name would be "Top of the World Trailhead." Looking around at the surrounding high country, it sure seems like the top of the world. In fact, the Top of the World Store is only 1 mile to the west. The trails start at 9,518 feet, and obviously, they can't climb too much from that point. Therefore, all trips starting from this trailhead are made-to-order for people who don't like big hills.

The trailhead is right in the middle of the uniquely beautiful Wyoming High Lakes country. It's hard to believe that this isn't officially part of the Absaroka-Beartooth Wilderness, but it's just as wild and the Forest Service manages it "to preserve its wilderness character." Backcountry travelers don't officially cross the wilderness boundary until they reach the Montana-Wyoming state line.

Dozens of lakes are found within a short walk of the trailhead. Even the trailhead itself is on the shores of magnificent Island Lake. The campground here is popular and usually full. Even the trailhead parking lot sometimes fills to capacity.

This trailhead is more suited to families and beginners than any trailhead in the Beartooths. The scenery is outstanding, yet exploring requires little effort. But keep in mind that these trails run at or above timberline in an alpine environment. The weather can change quickly and severely, so be watchful and prepared.

The hike: The trail is about as flat as it gets, but it's still one of the most scenic routes in the Beartooths. Depending on the time of year, you might have to get your feet wet crossing Little Bear Creek right at the trailhead. Later in the season, however, you can usually hop across the stream on exposed rocks.

From the trailhead the trail closely follows the west shore of Island Lake for most of the first mile. Then it leads less than 0.25 mile over to Night Lake and once again follows the west shore. Night Lake resembles Island Lake and the trail again closely follows the shoreline.

Small children love this section of trail, but they tend to go slow because there are so many discoveries for them to make.

Options: You can continue on, past Night Lake, to Flake Lake and even farther to Becker Lake. The way to Becker Lake is well defined, but it's not an official Forest Service trail, nor does it show up on the Forest Service or USGS maps.

Fishing information: Much of this area is easily accessible to horses, and as a result, many of the lakes were planted with brook trout in the first half of the century. The rationale was that brookies are hearty, easily reproduce, and could establish reproducing populations—which they did. Today, brookies provide excellent fishing for great numbers of aggressive, hungry trout. However, brookies tend to overpopulate these lakes, resulting in smaller fish. On the positive side, 8- to 9-inch brookies may be the tastiest trout of the Beartooths.

This trail originates in Wyoming, if you go far enough, it enters Montana. Those planning to fish here need to know where one state ends and the other begins. To fish in both states, obtain fishing licenses and regulations for both states.

Island and Night lakes have been stocked with rainbows, but now these two lakes are primarily brook trout fisheries. Becker Lake may hold some cutthroats that have migrated down from Albino Lake.

For some variety and a chance to hook cutthroat trout, head up over the saddle at the end of Becker Lake into Montana and Albino Lake. It is stocked on a four-year basis and has some natural reproduction as well to provide some variation in size.

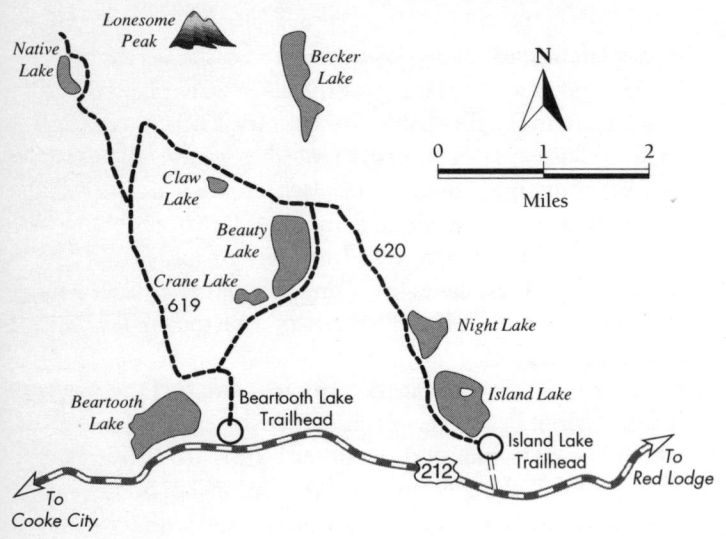

15
BEARTOOTH HIGH LAKES

> see map on page 48

Type of hike: Shuttle.
Total distance: 5.9 miles.
Maps: USGS, Beartooth Butte; RMS, Wyoming Beartooths.
Finding the trailhead: Refer to Night Lake (Hike 14) or Beauty Lake (Hike 16), depending on which way you take this shuttle hike.

Key points:
1.0   Night Lake.
2.5   Flake Lake.
3.2   Junction with Trail 621 to Beartooth Lake Trailhead.
3.3   Upper end of Beauty Lake.
4.3   Lower end of Beauty Lake.
4.5   Junction with trail to Crane Lake.
5.9   Beartooth Lake Trailhead.

Overview: The Island Lake and Beartooth Lake trailheads are in what is commonly called the Wyoming high lakes country. It's hard to believe that this isn't officially part of the Absaroka-Beartooth Wilderness, but it's just as wild and the Forest Service manages it "to preserve its wilderness character." Backcountry travelers don't officially cross the wilderness boundary until they reach the Montana-Wyoming state line.

Dozens of lakes are easy hikes from either trailhead, and both trailheads have wonderful vehicle campgrounds and picnic areas. The scenery is outstanding, yet exploring requires little effort. But keep in mind that these trails run at or above timberline in an alpine environment. The weather can change quickly and severely, so be watchful and prepared.

The hike: This trail is longer than most hikes in this book are, but it's an easy, flat walk with truly outstanding scenery.

This is one of those shuttle trails that requires arranging transportation in advance. Leave a vehicle at the Beartooth Lake Trailhead or arrange with another party to start at Beartooth Lake and meet along the trail for lunch so you can trade keys. The trail can be hiked from either direction with no extra difficulty, but this description starts at the Island Lake Trailhead.

Plan on taking the entire day to cover the distance, leaving plenty of time to enjoy the scenery. Carry a water filter to save weight rather than packing in several full water bottles; the route follows streams and lakes virtually every step of the way.

You might have to get your feet wet right after the trailhead where the trail crosses Little Bear Creek, which flows from Island Lake to Beartooth Lake. In August and September you might be able to walk across on rocks, but usually not in July.

After going along Island, Night, and Flake lakes, the trail turns west just after Flake Lake and soon drops down into Beauty Lake, where the scenery matches the name. Just before the lake, look for Trail 621 heading off to the south along the east shore of Beauty Lake. Turn left (south) at this junction.

For 1 mile, the trail follows the east shoreline of Beauty Lake. Shortly after leaving Beauty Lake, the trail goes by Crane Lake. This lake is worth the 100-yard side trail to relax by this scenic lake with a sandy shoreline.

From Crane Lake, it's a gradual downhill walk through mostly forested terrain to Beartooth Lake. You cross Little Bear Creek again just before reaching the trailhead. Instead of crossing where the trail hits the creek, follow a path to your left along the creek for about 50 yards where you might find a footbridge.

Options: If this hike isn't enough for you, it can be lengthened to 8.5 miles by continuing west on the Beartooth Hike Lakes Trail No. 620, turning left (south) at Trail No. 619, and then hiking to Beartooth Lake Trailhead

Fishing information: Fishing along this trail leans toward brook trout, although several other species have been planted over the brook trout populations. Fishing is usually excellent in lakes with brookies, but some days even these fish are hard to catch—and sometimes hardware users will out-fish the fly fishermen.

Beauty Lake has had cutts stocked over the brookies. Claw, Horseshoe, and Beartooth lakes have all had lake trout planted to feed on the brookies to control their population. Beartooth Lake has had several other species introduced, including rainbows, cutts, goldens, and grayling.

16
BEAUTY LAKE

see map on page 48

Type of hike: Out and back.
Total distance: 3.2 miles.
Maps: USGS, Beartooth Butte; RMS, Wyoming Beartooths.
Finding the trailhead: From Cooke City, drive east about 23 miles on U.S. Highway 212 to a well-marked turnoff for Beartooth Lake Campground. From Red Lodge it's about 40 miles west of Red Lodge—and about 1 mile west of the Top of the World Store. Once in the campground, it might take a few minutes to find the trailhead. The likely looking spot on the left just past the entrance is actually a picnic area and boat launch. The trailhead is at the north end of the campground.

But it might be best to park in the lot at the picnic area near the entrance to the campground. The last 100 yards to the trailhead is rough, and the parking area right at the trailhead is small and not well suited for passenger cars.

Key points:
0.2 Junction with trail to Beauty Lake.
1.4 Junction with trail to Crane Lake.
1.6 South edge of Beauty Lake.
2.4 Junction with Beartooth High Lakes Trail 620.

Overview: As at Island Lake, the Beartooth Lake Trailhead sits on the edge of a large mountain lake, and the trails start right at the Beartooth Lake Campground. Hikers can camp right at the trailhead and get an early start on the first day—if they are fortunate enough to find a campsite in the popular campground.

Beartooth Lake lies in the shadow of famous 10,514-foot Beartooth Butte, which dominates the western horizon. Beartooth Butte is an enigma, a tiny island of sedimentary rock in a sea of granite making up the Beartooth Mountains. Geologists aren't completely sure how this happened, but they do know that Beartooth Butte contains fossils of some the oldest known plants ever found in North America. Unlike Island Lake, however, the Beartooth Lake Trailhead parking area is small and at the end of a rough road.

The hike: This trail leaves from a major vehicle campground and is one of the most accessible trails in the Beartooths. Consequently, the trail to Beauty Lake receives heavy use—compared to most other trails in the Beartooths, but not heavy compared to short day hikes in most national parks.

After crossing Little Bear Creek on a footbridge by the trailhead, hike along the stream for about 100 yards until you see the trail heading off to the right through a meadow. The trail can get faint here, but it becomes well defined on the other side of the meadow and stays that way all the way to Beauty Lake.

In less than 0.25 mile after the trailhead, the trail splits. Trail 619 veers off to the left toward Beartooth Butte. Go right on Trail 621 to Beauty Lake.

A gradual climb of about 500 feet leads through lush forest with lots of wildflowers and mushrooms. The trail is rocky in a few places, but is still nicely suited for families with small children. It's rare for such great scenery to grace such a short hike.

The trail climbs gradually to Beauty Lake, but it's all downhill on the way back to the trailhead.

At 1.4 miles, look for Crane Lake off to the left (west) and a spur trail splitting off toward the lake. Crane Lake might not be your destination, but it's nice enough to be. The lake has a sandy shoreline, rare in the Beartooths.

After checking out Crane Lake, take the right fork in the trail and continue north for less than 0.25 mile to Beauty Lake. All visitors probably agree that this lake lives up to its name. This large, clear, alpine lake boasts several sandy beaches just right for wading on a warm day.

Fishing information: This trailhead is in Wyoming. Those planning to fish need to know where one state ends and the other begins. To fish in both states, carry licenses and regulations for both states.

Beartooth Lake has been stocked with lake trout, which have thinned the brook trout population. The remaining brookies are larger than average size. Beartooth Lake has had several introductions of other species including rainbows, cutts, goldens, and grayling.

Even though other species have been planted in Beauty Lake, the fishing is still dominated by brook trout. Crane Lake has had cutts stocked over the brookies. Fishing in both lakes is excellent.

17
CLAW LAKE

see map on page 48

Type of hike: Loop.
Total distance: 8.3 miles.
Maps: USGS, Beartooth Butte, RMS, Wyoming Beartooths.
Finding the trailhead: Refer to Beauty Lake, Hike 16.

Key points:
- 0.2 Junction with Trail 621 to Beauty lake. Bear left.
- 2.9 Junction with Beartooth High Lakes Trail 620.
- 3.9 Horseshoe Lake.
- 4.1 Marmot Lake.
- 4.3 Shallow Lake.
- 4.7 Claw Lake.
- 5.9 Junction with Trail 621. Bear right.
- 6.7 South end of Beauty Lake.
- 6.9 Crane Lake.
- 8.3 Beartooth Lake Trailhead.

Overview: Refer to Beauty Lake, Hike 16.

The hike: This trip works either clockwise or counter-clockwise, but clockwise seems slightly easier. There are five more stream crossings on this hike, but it's usually possible to cross on rocks and keep your feet dry.

After crossing Little Bear Creek on a footbridge by the trailhead, hike along the stream for about 100 yards until you see the trail heading off to the right through a meadow. The trail can get faint here, but it becomes well defined on the other side of the meadow.

Less than 0.25 mile from the trailhead, watch for the junction with Trail 621 to Beauty Lake. To do this trip clockwise, turn left to stay on Trail 619 and head for Beartooth Butte. The return route of this loop comes down Trail 621 to this junction on the final leg to the trailhead.

The first part of the trail hugs the north shoreline of beautiful Beartooth Lake. Some parts of the trail can get quite marshy, especially in June and July. Then, after crossing Beartooth Creek, the trail turns north through the shadow of spectacular Beartooth Butte for another 2 miles to the junction with Beartooth High Lakes Trail 620.

Turn right (east) onto the Beartooth High Lakes Trail and don't be surprised when the trail fades away for about 0.25 mile. A series of cairns clearly marks the way. At the top of a small ridge (the highest point on this trail, about 9,900 feet), the trail becomes well defined again. From this point onto Claw Lake, the trail skirts the south edge of a chain of lakes. Beyond the lakes to the north looms awesome, 11,409-foot Lonesome Mountain.

Continue 1 mile down the trail to Claw Lake. From Claw Lake, it's slightly more than 1 mile to the junction with Trail 621, which heads south along the east shore of Beauty Lake and past Crane Lake back to the Beartooth Lake Trailhead. Drop your pack at this junction and walk over to the rocky ledge on the north end of Beauty Lake for a fantastic view of the well-named lake. This is a great place to eat lunch for day hikers on this loop. There are several more views to equal this one farther along the lake's edge.

Fishing information: Claw, Horseshoe, and Beartooth lakes have all been planted with lake trout to act as predators to the brook trout populations. For the most part, the fishing along this route is the standard brook trout fare. Sorry, there aren't any grayling left in Grayling Lake.

18
NATIVE LAKE

see map on page 48

Type of hike: Out-and-back or shuttle.
Total distance: 8 miles.
Maps: USGS, Beartooth Butte, Muddy Creek, Castle Mountain, and Silver Run Peak; RMS, Wyoming Beartooths and Alpine–Mount Maurice.
Finding the trailhead: Refer to Beauty Lake, Hike 16.

Key points:
0.2   Junction with Trail 621 to Beauty Lake, bear left.
2.9   Junction with Beartooth High Lakes Trail 620, bear left.
3.6   Turn off to Clay Butte Trailhead.
4.0   Native Lake.

Overview: Refer to Beauty Lake, Hike 16.

The hike: How to get to Native Lake can be a tough decision. Going in at the Beartooth Lake Trailhead, as described in this book, is the shortest way. But the Clay Butte and Island Lake trailheads also offer access to this area.

Regardless of which trailhead you use, the way into Native Lake can be nearly effortless compared to many trails in the Beartooths. All three trails go through gorgeous, open, alpine country, dotted with lakes and carpeted with wildflowers.

After crossing Little Bear Creek on a footbridge by the trailhead, hike along the stream for about 100 yards until you see the trail heading off to the right through a meadow. Less than 0.25 mile from the trailhead, watch for the junction with Trail 621 to Beauty Lake. Turn left to stay on Trail 619 and head for Beartooth Butte.

Start out hiking around the north edge of Beartooth Lake on the edge of some moist meadows. Beartooth Butte provides a magnificent backdrop on the western horizon most of the way into Native Lake. The trail crosses Beartooth Creek twice, but it's usually easy to find a way across on rocks without getting your feet wet.

At the junction with Beartooth High Lakes Trail 620, bear left and keep going north on Trail 619. About 0.5 mile after the junction, watch for a trail and a string of cairns going off to the west through the pass on the north side of Beartooth Butte. These cairns lead down to Trail 614 to Clay Butte.

Continue northwest on the main trail another 0.5 mile to Native Lake. The trail is well defined the entire way.

From Native Lake, there are plenty of options for adventurous side trips. This is a great place to practice using a compass and topo map.

Options: Consider arranging a shuttle at a different trailhead to avoid retracing your steps on the way out. With two vehicles, it's best to leave a vehicle at Beartooth Lake (8,900 feet elevation) and go in at the Clay Butte Trailhead (9,600 feet elevation).

Fishing information: Native Lake is a cutthroat exception to the brook trout theme found throughout this area. If the cutts are being stubborn, many of the lakes in the area sport voracious populations of brookies. The nearby Beartooth High Lakes Trail provides access to many of these, with lake trout having been added to both T and Lamb lakes. The Montana state line is about 1 mile north of Native Lake, so anglers must make sure they have the proper state license.

19
CRAZY CREEK FALLS

Type of hike: Out-and-back.
Total distance: 1 mile.
Maps: USGS, Jim Smith Peak; RMS, Wyoming Beartooths.

Finding the trailhead: The Crazy Lake Trailhead is 10.7 miles east of Cooke City on the Beartooth Highway (U.S. Highway 212). The trailhead is a turnoff on the north side of the highway across from the Crazy Creek Campground.

Overview: Crazy Creek is the trailhead that everybody drives by on their way to more popular trails that leave from the Cooke City, Beartooth Lake, or Island Lake trailheads. All those who drive by are missing something.

The Crazy Lakes area is drier and more forested than the high-altitude areas, but it's just as wild and beautiful. And it definitely receives much less use than the more popular trails. The area around the trailhead is not within the Absaroka-Beartooth Wilderness.

The hike: The centerpiece of the area, Crazy Creek Falls, is only a short walk from the trailhead. Even if you don't take a longer foray up Crazy Creek, do stop for a few minutes to savor the raw beauty of Crazy Creek Falls.

You can hear the falls right from the trailhead and after walking up the trail about 100 feet, you can see this massive cascade. The trail continues along the falls for about 0.5 mile with several great viewpoints of the falls. If you stop to see Crazy Creek Falls in June, you'll be amazed on how much water is tumbling out of the mountains.

Options: You can continue up the trail to Ivy Lake, but this is a 9-mile, out-and-back trip.

Crazy Creek Falls

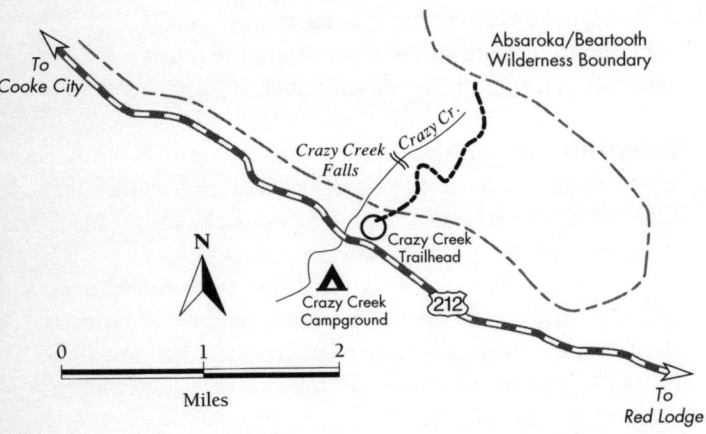

20
KERSEY LAKE

Type of hike: Out-and-back.
Total distance: 3 miles.
Maps: USGS, Black Pyramid Mountain; RMS, Alpine–Mount Maurice.
Finding the trailhead: Take U.S. Highway 212 east from Cooke City for 4.2 miles and turn left (north) onto Forest Road 306. Drive about 0.5 mile to the trailhead. Trail 3 takes off at the far end of this large trailhead and parking area.

Key points:
0.5   Junction with Kersey Lake Jeep Road.
1.2   Junction with Lake Vernon Trail 565.
1.5   East shore of Kersey Lake.

Overview: Anyone who has been to the Clarks Fork Trailhead could mount a strong argument that it's the most beautiful trailhead in the Beartooths. It rests on the south shoreline of the Clarks Fork of the Yellowstone as the river leaves the Beartooths right at a spectacular falls and large pool. The large grassy area with picnic tables is especially nice for people wanting a leisurely picnic in a gorgeous setting followed by a short day hike. In fact, a worthwhile attraction lies just beyond the trailhead, where a major footbridge spans the Clarks Fork where it has cut a narrow gorge.

Since this trailhead is the south end of "The Beaten Path" through the Beartooths, it's obviously heavily used. It's also large, with toilet facilities and plenty of room to park or turn around any vehicle. Visitors might find twenty vehicles parked here, possibly from twenty different states.

Backcountry horsemen use a companion trailhead just west of the main trailhead, also with a well-signed turnoff along the Beartooth Highway about 0.25 mile to the west. This is the only trailhead in the Beartooths where the Forest Service has provided separate facilities for backcountry horseman and hikers

Also check out the watchable wildlife interpretive display put up by the Forest Service. It's located on the Beartooth Highway between the entrances to the two trailheads.

The hike: To find Kersey Lake, take Trail 3 from the Clarks Fork Trailhead. Immediately after leaving the trailhead, you cross an awe-inspiring wooden footbridge over the Clarks Fork of the Yellowstone where it gushes through a narrow gorge.

The first mile of the trail is split—the east path is for hikers and the west for horses. After about 0.5 mile, turn right (east) at the well-marked junction with the Kersey Lake jeep road.

From this point, it's about another mile to the east shore of massive Kersey Lake. Just before you reach the lake, the trail to Lake Vernon veers off to the right (east).

There are cabins with vehicle access to the south shore of the lake. These are private inholdings; one is a Forest Service rental cabin. Kersey Lake is not within the Absaroka-Beartooth Wilderness.

Kersey Lake, Lake Vernon, Rock Island Lake

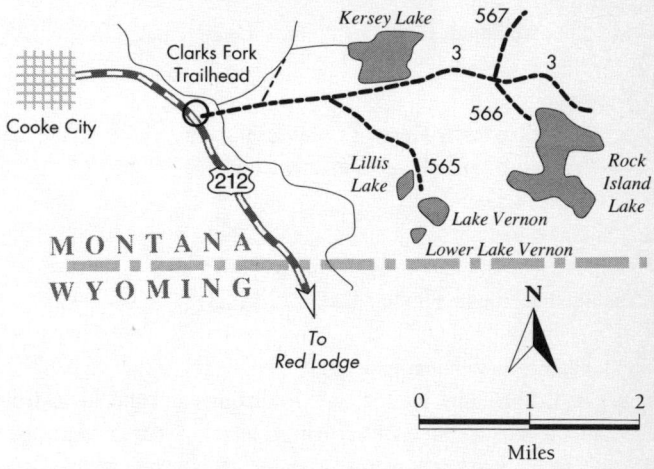

21
LAKE VERNON

> see map on page 65

Type of hike: Out-and-back.
Total distance: 5 miles.
Maps: USGS, Fossil Lake; RMS, Cooke City-Cutoff Mountain.
Finding the trailhead: Refer to Kersey Lake, Hike 20.

Key points:
0.5 Junction with Kersey Lake jeep road.
1.2 Junction with Lake Vernon Trail 565.
1.8 Lillis Lake.
1.1 Lake Vernon.

Overview: Refer to Kersey Lake, Hike 20.

The hike: Lake Vernon is a great choice for a day hike with small children. The trail is well maintained and easy to follow all the way as it passes through a rich, unburned forest. Keep a sharp eye out for moose, especially in the big meadow just before Lillis Lake.

The trail doesn't have abundant drinking water, so bring an extra bottle. Like all trails in this area, mosquitoes can be bothersome, especially early in the summer.

To reach Lake Vernon, take Trail 3 from the Clarks Fork Trailhead for about 1.2 miles to a well-signed junction with Trail 564 to Lake Vernon. Turn right (south) and head up a moderate grade. After another 0.5 mile or so look for little, jewel-like Lillis Lake in the foreground with majestic Pilot Peak and Index Peak as a backdrop.

The trail continues around the northwest shoreline of Lillis Lake less than a mile more to the destination, Lake Vernon. This forest-lined lake is larger than Lillis but offers a similar view of Pilot and Index. Just south of Lake Vernon is Lower Lake Vernon, more appropriately called Reed Lake on some maps since it's little more than a scenic marsh.

On the way out of Lake Vernon, the trail climbs the biggest hill of the trip, about 0.5 mile long. Once at the top, however, it's downhill all the way to the trailhead.

Fishing information: This short day hike offers some surprising fishing. Brook trout have trouble reproducing in Lillis Lake, and the smaller population translates into bigger brookies. Be sure to stop at this small lake on the way to Vernon, which hosts both cutthroat and brook trout. Just over the hill, you could find yourself alone catching stocked cutthroats at Margaret Lake.

22
ROCK ISLAND LAKE

> see map on page 65

Type of hike: Out-and-back.
Total distance: 6 miles.
Maps: USGS, Fossil Lake; RMS, Cooke City-Cutoff Mountain.
Finding the trailhead: Refer to Kersey Lake, Hike 20.

Key points:
0.5 Junction with Kersey Lake jeep road.
1.2 Junction with Trail 565 to Lake Vernon.
1.5 Kersey Lake.
2.4 Junction with Trail 565 to Rock Island Lake.
3.0 Rock Island Lake.

Overview: Refer to Kersey Lake, Hike 20.

The hike: Rock Island Lake differs from many high-elevation lakes. Instead of forming a small, concise oval in the end of a cirque, it sprawls through flat and forested terrain, seemingly branching off in every direction. Visitors can spend an entire day just walking around it.

To get to Rock Island Lake, take Trail 3 from the Clarks Fork Trailhead to the junction with Trail 565 to Rock Island Lake. Turn right (east) here for about another 0.5 mile to the lake. The trail is well used and well maintained the entire way with only one hill (near Kersey Lake). The 1988 fires scorched the area around Kersey Lake but missed Rock Island Lake.

Because Rock Island Lake is so accessible and easy to reach (3 miles on a near-level trail), it's a perfect choice for a family planning their first trip into the Absaroka-Beartooth Wilderness. Drinking water is readily available on the trail and at the lake (it must be boiled or filtered), but the mosquitoes are bad in early summer.

Fishing information: This popular lake has a combination of homegrown brookies and cutthroats stocked on a three-year rotation, both of which grow well in this lake. The fishing should generally be good enough to count on for dinner.

23
LADY OF THE LAKE

Type of hike: Out-and-back.
Total distance: 3 miles.
Maps: USGS, Cooke City; RMS, Cooke City-Cutoff Mountain.

Finding the trailhead: To reach the trailhead from Cooke City, drive east on U.S. Highway 212 for 3.2 miles to a turnoff marked with a large Forest Service sign as the Goose Lake jeep road, just before the Colter Campground. Turn north off U.S. Highway 212 and drive northeast about 2 miles up this gravel road to a cluster of old buildings. An inconspicuous trailhead on the right shoulder of the road has an old Forest Service sign for Lady of the Lake. The 2 miles of road to the trailhead are passable with any vehicle, but to continue up the road past the trailhead for any reason a high-clearance vehicle is essential.

Overview: This trailhead is slightly harder to locate than most others in the Beartooths, but this hasn't lessened its popularity. The area has lots to offer, and it receives heavy use both by locals and those who travel from afar for a chance to experience this spectacular wild area.

The trailhead lies on the eastern fringe of the section of the Beartooths that has been extensively mined, logged, and roaded. Even in the 2 miles of gravel road to the trailhead, the contrast between this area and the pristine wilderness is clearly evident. You can camp at the undeveloped campground at the trailhead to get an earlier start.

The hike: Lady of the Lake is an ideal choice for an easy day hike with small children. Besides being a short hike, the weather isn't as critical as it is at the higher elevations.

Unfortunately, hikers might have to get their feet wet immediately upon starting this trip. The bridge over Fisher

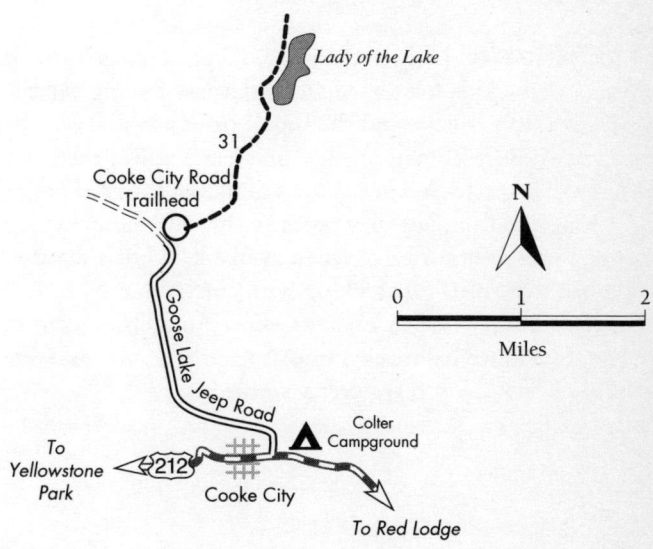

Creek washed out years ago, and until late in the year, the stream carries too much water to ford without wading.

After Fisher Creek, the trail goes by a small private inholding with a cabin, and then heads down a well-maintained, forest-lined trail to Lady of the Lake. The Forest Service sign says 1 mile to the lake, but it's probably more like 1.5 miles. The trail breaks out of the trees in the large marshy meadow at the foot of the lake.

This is a heavily used area, with some major wear and tear along the trail on the west shore of the lake.

The return trip involves more climbing than the way in, so allow extra time, especially if traveling with small children.

Fishing information: Lady of the Lake is a personal favorite of places to take kids for their first wilderness fishing experience. The hike is easy, and the brook trout are always willing. For those with some wilderness experience, there are four small lakes nestled in the trees to the southeast. They're a bit tough to find, but they promise solitude. Grayling are stocked in Mosquito Lake when available, while the other lakes are scheduled for stocking with cutthroats.

Don't bother to fish Fisher Creek. Acid effluent from mines abandoned before environmental protection laws were in place keeps this stream pretty sterile.

About The Author

Whenever Bill Schneider isn't out in the wilderness, he wants to be. He has spent over 30 years hiking trails all across America.

During college in the late 1960s, he worked on a trail crew in Glacier National Park. Then, he spent the 1970s publishing the *Montana Outdoors Magazine* for the Montana Department of Fish, Wildlife & Parks and covering as many miles of trails as possible on weekends and holidays.

In 1979, Bill, along with his partner, Mike Sample, created Falcon Press Publishing and released two guidebooks the first year. Bill wrote one of them, *Hiking Montana*, which is still a popular guidebook. Since then, he has also written twelve more books and many magazine articles on wildlife, outdoor recreation, and environmental issues. Along the way, on a part-time basis over a span of 12 years, Bill has taught classes on bicycling, backpacking, no-trace camping, and hiking in bear country for The Yellowstone Institute, a nonprofit educational organization in Yellowstone National Park.

Since 1979, Bill has served as publisher of Falcon Publishing, which is now established as a premier publisher of recreational guidebooks with more than 350 titles in print.

All books in this popular series are 6x9", regularly updated with accurate information on access, side trips, & safety.

HIKING GUIDES

Hiking Alaska
Hiking Alberta
Hiking Arizona
Hiking Arizona's Catcus Country
Hiking the Beartooths
Hiking Big Bend National Park
Hiking California
Hiking California's Desert Parks
Hiking Carlsbad Caverns &
    Guadalupe Mnts. National Parks
Hiking Colorado
Hiking the Columbia River Gorge
Hiking Florida
Hiking Georgia
Hiking Glacier/Waterton Lakes
    National Parks
Hiking Grand Canyon National Park
Hiking Great Basin
Hiking Hot Springs
    in the Pacific Northwest
Hiking Idaho
Hiking Maine
Hiking Michigan
Hiking Minnesota
Hiking Montana
Hiking Nevada
Hiking New Hampshire
Hiking New Mexico
Hiking New York
Hiking North Carolina
Hiking North Cascades
Hiking Northern Arizona
Hiking Olympic National Park
Hiking Oregon
Hiking Oregon's Eagle Cap Wilderness
Hiking Oregon's Three Sisters Country
Hiking Pennsylvania
Hiking South Carolina
Hiking South Dakota's Black Hills Country
Hiking Southern New England
Hiking Tennessee
Hiking Texas
Hiking Utah
Hiking Utah's Summits
Hiking Vermont
Hiking Virginia
Hiking Washington
Hiking Wyoming
Hiking Wyoming's Wind River Range
Hiking Yellowstone National Park
Hiking Zion & Bryce Canyon National Parks
Exploring Canyonlands & Arches National
    Parks
The Trail Guide to Bob Marshall Country

BEST EASY DAY HIKES

Beartooths
Canyonlands & Arches
Continental Divide
Glacier & Waterton Lakes
Glen Canyon
Grand Canyon
North Cascades
Yellowstone

MORE THAN 4 MILLION COPIES SOLD!